This Diet of Flesh

poems by

Scott Honeycutt

Finishing Line Press
Georgetown, Kentucky

This Diet of Flesh

For Nora and Rose

ACKNOWLEDGMENTS

Fresh Breath: "Atlas," "Home on December 1st," "In the Peach Orchard,"
Mississippi River Poetry Anthology: "The Burial of Hernando de Soto, May 1542,"
"The Palisades"
Kindred Magazine: "Brushing My Young Daughter's Hair"
Torrid Literature Journal: "Flint River, Georgia"
Anthology of Appalachian Writers, Homer Hickam Volume VII: "Sand Mountain"
Deep South Magazine: "The Night It Happened"

Editor: Christen Kincaid

Cover Art: Ralph E. Johnston IV, www.johnstonartdesign.com

Author Photo: Rebecca Honeycutt

Cover Design: Elizabeth Maines

Printed in the USA on acid-free paper.
Order online: www.finishinglinepress.com
also available on amazon.com

Author inquiries and mail orders:
Finishing Line Press
P. O. Box 1626
Georgetown, Kentucky 40324
U. S. A.

Table of Contents

Part One:
A Coiled Message

Sand Mountain

After Noah docked his barge
on the summit of Sand Mountain,
Alabama,
he opened its dark hold and found
it full of cleave-eyed serpents.
The Old World menagerie of
beasts that had boarded so long ago
were transmuted in passage
into these coiled, taut messengers
of deliverance.

At the end of our days what
remains if not praise and conviction?
So why not take up snakes after
the heaving waters leave us on
hard land and offer a rainbow
full of scales alive with God?

Flint River, Georgia

One June morning near the close
of the twentieth century, two friends
found a three hundred-year-old
hand-dug canoe in a muddy bank by
the Flint River. No one knows
how many times it had worked its
leverage down the Flint's glossy
mill before becoming marooned and
forgotten between the water's edge
and sand heaps. The Flint keeps
its secret passages and gives only
those artifacts back to the living
that the river has used up.
It is as if the shoals had posed some
improbable question years before
and now were compelled to deliver an
answer, spoken only in the mute canoe's
silent dialogue between an unquenched
river and those untidy Georgia hills.

The Palisades

My old fishing buddy, Chadwick, once told me
how he stood on the Palisades above the river
and watched a thick-chested merman pull his
weight backward down the Mississippi. From this high
place, the merman's wake seemed to pour out from
beneath his corded arms as the strokes and flap of his
sturgeon tail arched out in a giant splash-plume of
American toil. Who is to say what legions still
populate these brown waters? Perhaps the blue heron
hunting down there has seen him, too, stroking his
frothy locks and sunning on a sandbar at noon.

The Burial of Hernando de Soto, May 1542

No moon appeared on the night that
Hernando de Soto was dropped like a soft anchor deep into
the Mississippi River.
He and his Spanish brothers had spent seasons troubling across
this green continent searching for El Dorado,
but here, fever-dead and unaware, de Soto lost all interest.

He was wrapped in a loose shroud and ferried out into the water.
His grim crew burned pitch-torches to his memory,
so their flotilla of canoes flickered in darkness.
When de Soto's slender fingers slipped from under the cloth
and dipped into the cool water, somewhere his iron soul
must have shivered, feeling the golden halls envelop around him
as a ruby-eyed catfish reeled up from its depths.

Basho's Complaint, June 8th

Walking along the Chattooga River one morning after skies
opened and drowned out our camp,
it was impossible to hear anything other than whitewater
churning on rocks below.
The slick trail throve green in the night and mossed-out
a tapered pathway. Wet laurel leaves exploded and quickened,
growing flush against the Appalachian jungle,
and sunk like granite into the bottom of my pack
there lay a translation of Basho's *Narrow Road to the Deep North*.
I had hoped to learn something from the master,
something concerning pleasures of privation or blooms of solitude.
But now my mood became full of the West.

The book's sodden, heavy pages leaked ink and labored
together so that feudal Japan moved from poetry
to abstraction to mere weight.
To lighten my load, I reached in beneath the camp stove
and sleeping pad and tugged out old Basho by the ear.
He frowned like a withered toad, occupied with his own trouble.
I left him there to dry on a stone in South Carolina,
where he could count stars or haunt holy shrines while waiting
for some other traveler to lug him up from the gorge.

Our pursuits of enlightenment are so causally disregarded—
like love's tallow, dripping from clouds of our hidden, mizzling days.

Walking the Dog into the Summer Solstice

It must have been earth's leaning axis that pushed us out of doors.
My dog with his cosmic nose full of summer's long light
led us off into an evening that smelled of rain
and backyard cooking.
We walked up Lynnwood Drive, unstitching ourselves from
indoor concerns. The asphalt's tar stretched
out beyond our normal route into *unnosed* territory,
where poison ivy snakes up the side of poplar trees that bend
across the road. The next storm might overtake them at last.

We rambled on past empty soccer fields and playgrounds
out toward the alleys of Unaka Avenue, gauging twilight's
drop by speeding cars that steadily switched on their lights.
Each sighing house was a tableau filled with the loves and
hates of our entirety.
The bluing air gathered up those frames and propelled
silhouettes that streaked from room to room—now frozen,
now moving—backlit against the burn of televisions and lamps.
Bicycles with deflated tires lay across the lawns, waiting
for ghost-riders to return.

Then somewhere, miles from home, my dog's wet nose
came to full stop deep within a boxwood hedge.
Out bolted a rabbit that cross-stitched the grass
and jolted between emerging fireflies,
charting out the diagrams of their fleeting constellations.
When at last it plunged through a drainage pipe,
dozens of those illuminations closed in around the hole.

And suddenly, there it was—the unseen, intractable *Night*.

Home on December 1st

The lake tonight is like a Flemish tapestry,
dark and faded against the sky.
It drifts in its weave. Dipped, curled,
and swirled in liquid cords, its lilt
braves up toward the flicking porch lights
that glow near the shore.

If I were a suicide, I would make my
selfish claim here among the cattails
and silt.

So beautiful is she tonight.
Silent as an abbey.

In the distance, four geese land and
a fisherman checks his line
as the moon strolls out into his
yard of stars.

In the Peach Orchard

The peach blossoms roused early this year,
so all through the orchard, keepers
measured their steps, counting the blooming
trees against those whose slumbers still
held the autumn drop.
I walked here among the pink profusion,
listening for migratory birds whose
wings gauge seasons and whose songs
sound like the piping of the globe.

What is human love set against this unfolding
of mystic energy? How can we define
these acres of flesh-like flowers that
burst and smell so unforeseen and unexpected,
though each year I come pleading their
arrival like a lover who pines
below a woman's opened window
as her eyes close around the silver horns
of the moon?

After Reading Charles Wright, I Drive Out to His Childhood Home

Chestnut Ridge rises like hands folded in prayer above
Kingsport, Tennessee. It's midnight,
and I wind up the rim on Old Stage Road in
a fog searching.
I shouldn't be here—out attending another man's
memories when I've a stable of my own back at home.
Yet here I am: thick-knuckling the wheel, driving back
and forth in front of his darkened ancestral home
like I've put time in an ossuary, yet I'm calling it out to play.

The radio's off its dial—a shock of whiteness scans the road.
To the north, old Clinch Mountain is still the same.
It slaps its shadow across the valley weathering it all.
Above, the stars, if I could see them, are still the same.
And below, the glow of Kingsport blinks out like a thousand
lighthouse flames.
It's so clear though:
Reading has done nothing for my soul.

Atlas

Tennessee stretches out like the figure of a man dreaming.
His head pillows between mountains and ridgelines,
And his feet soak in the broad, flowing river.

Part II:
Dark Question, No Reply

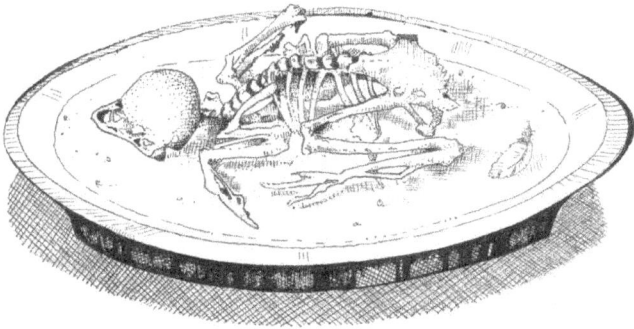

The Knowing

The first time we touched after her shared
experiences with other men's prided histories,
I lay next to her and heard the gilded applause,
the happy message that so many could be content
in her body and live on this diet of flesh
like jackals gladdened from a hunt's red offal.

I studied them, four shadows, a uniformed heat,
flickering against the bed. They hovered in unison,
amnesiac from each other yet united by me.
I shuddered as they spread dim thighs and made
semen whisk, populating memory with their rallied cries.

What are these still moments rounding our branded lives?
I ask again, *what is man?*
Must he suffer these beasts to intrude on this most private
and unfortunate of knowing?

Elegy for Wanda, an English Teacher

When you stepped into dawn that morning with
your hair up in ribbons and a pink bathrobe
brushed open exposing the gown underneath,
you seemed so much younger than your grief.
If not for the missing slipper or the dazzled look of
lost stars pocketed in your eyes,
you may have been a heroine gliding out of the nineteenth
century to meet a lover, there beyond the camellia hedge.

But on that day, no one could have imagined your intent
as you peered up and watched the moon and sun
fuse into one golden ring.
You must have paused under the two, a broken fulcrum
who had the power to weigh and stop time.

Too many books with heavy themes,
Too many pages that fanned and floated into the last chapter,
always asking some unsolvable yet beautiful question.
When they found you in the late afternoon, between the freshly
dug mums and the patio, your face held a delighted expression
like a southern girl who witnesses snowfall from the window of
her red-bricked room.

What Comes

In the years before it happened,
the house was like a guarded keep,
where memories sipped from teacups
and roses grew thorny in sleep.
Dust had crazed the furniture,
and none of her children would phone.
Even her mind had left her,
when it realized she was dancing alone.

But now on the day of deliverance,
they come with baggage in hand
to fumble through her keepsakes
and tiptoe across the sand.
Through room after room they wander,
filling all hallways with light
as they brush past the form in the corner,
keeping it safe from sight.

Well into the night it continues,
the party and the whole affair.
There's a coroner out counting his silver,
a professional of despair.
Once she's all sorted and numbered,
she's stowed like a safe in the back.
A long car pulls from the driveway,
 and tires speed out toward the black.

Death's Pickpocket

Yesterday, I read about a man who awoke from death
just as his embalmment was underway.
As the formaldehyde needle pricked his skin, those eyes
unlocked.
No one was more surprised than the mortician
robbed of honest work.
Papers read "Miracle" and "Most True,"
yet I wonder how the man felt, raising stiff legs to walk
again
and breathing in the stale air of the butcher's room.

Charon's copper face must have grown slack
when he realized that his paddles in their one-way wake
must bend the inky waters
and turn and travel back across the blank space
toward the loud harbor moored there above.

On Discovering that My Ancestors Owned Hundreds of Slaves

Until recently, I aligned the past with my father's people.
They were hill-folk who came from England as indentured servants
before trading Virginia's tidewater
for the berms of Yancey County, North Carolina, where ridges
snipe upward and the moon is only viewed by looking straight above.
Once in the mountains, they grew independent and lean,
coveting bottomlands and the golden cut of tobacco priming.

I've learned, however, that many on mother's side kept on in the Old Dominion.
    After their release from indenture,
        they marketed their way into the planter class,
    purchasing land and seizing flat acres that needed toil.
        Of course, they bought African hands to grip the plows.
    Untold numbers of brown and black knuckles butchered hogs
        behind the hummock-gardens as others waited on the call
        of some slippered-foot to order their day.
Later, parts of the family migrated to Texas, pushing their lorded loads
        across an expanding range of southern peculiarity.

Truth always surprises:
One morning I walked along a peninsula between the James and York Rivers
and sliced my hand on a blade of marsh grass.
The blood was not immediate.
The skin merely opened up and hung there, a cut too sharp to feel.
What I believed was supple turned out to be scythe-like, crouching by the rivers,
waiting for the faintest touch.

Like Every Morning

Like every morning, he awoke at sunrise
To burden his face with the usual
Rituals of his condition. First, he
Lathered the cream and pulled a razor
Across his cheeks. Then he washed off the
Mint-smelling stuff and stepped out
Of his robe, leaving the night coiled
There on the tile. He had known the
Flushing of a half century, so when
He moved across the shower's edge and
Caught sight of his father's ass there in the
Corner of the mirror, he wasn't shocked.
It was neither revelation nor expected visitation.
He greeted his body like one who finds
A parcel of out-of-date coupons stored in
An old jacket pocket.
"So there it is." He might have said.
But no words came, just the pause, a moment
Really, no longer.
His eyes still held the shade of accusatory
Blue
That once had made each morning spruce.
Not much changes if the eyes
Can still project their will, he thought.

It was not sadness that he courted because
These private moments, before
The trappings of coffee and percolation
And before the gathering of clothes
Layered his life into the storehouse of expected
Behavior, were his alone.
There in the shower, as water streamed
Across his body, he absorbed the heat
And felt a tawny animal move somewhere in the
Forest.
Again, he almost spoke.
He knew, however, without question,
Those hooves would pound again sometime,
If not tomorrow then the next,
Like every morning.

Sharps Chapel

For Jesse Graves

I've been there once.
Dropping south out of the Cumberland Gap
Tunnel, my mother and I took a wrong turn
on our way home from Indianapolis, where we had
attempted to steal my brother back from himself.

It was Super Bowl Sunday.
The roads were emptied but still wet from a day
stocked with rain. The clouds, now loaded with night,
began to nuzzle in between ridges and broken
hills, yawning down to sleep just above Norris Lake,
not to rise until morning. I couldn't bear to tell her that
we were lost.

So I drove on.

We were in it before I knew we were on it: mid-century's
Maynardville Bridge enclosed around us like dread.
As we passed over, its welded brogues creaked through
riveted lattice works that thumped onto the steel deck,
strong enough to hold one more crossing, perhaps,
also willing, though, to drop at the next cough.

Once we were over it,
I confessed that we'd have to turn around
and drive back north under the trusses to where the
highway bent toward home.

We approached again, slowly, and I could see out across the
lake.
On a bluff above us,

house lights spilled down onto the cold water and seeped
out, sculpting the fog.

Halfway across it, I felt the drowned river's current
still flowing below the lake's surface, tiding fish and mussels
back and forth along their ancient channel.
When my car lights revealed the bridge's braced ribs,
green and rusted paint peeled from each terrace.
It rasped like a dragon dying.
Once over, I accelerated up a hill, and the bridge dropped
back into its dream.

Cresting the top, we spotted a roadside marker
that read *Welcome to Sharps Chapel.*
We must have slipped by it on our decent.
All around those words, the white sign winked through
the gloom, and sutured our fragmented map
that roved those distances between of hearth and heart.
To be received by spirits, to be pulled by sharp language
and welcomed back from the brink, that's all we can hope on this side
of the shore.

And it's often like this, I suppose, signs that clarify
our angles of repose remain hidden
when first passed.
Only after we've spooked ourselves into a grave
and dredged across it twice, can we know
then what darkness really asked.
So by twice going but once seen, we can trace that deeper road
ever and ever into the quiet, but faintly humming, night.

Brushing My Young Daughter's Hair

I am ill-equipped for such a task.
Even the way I grip the brush is
Off joint.
Like a carpenter's rafter in need of leveling,
I fumble with the brush, arm akimbo,
In lightening strokes of uneven flashes
That make shadows against the borrowed light
Of morning.

None of us are worthy of our creations,
And her hair, glistening with the innovations
Of blond youth, makes me understand
Gospel and adds a minute more
Of needed belief to the day.

The Night It Happened

On January 6, 2012, in Seminole County, Florida, a 3,500 year old bald cypress known as The Senator was torched by a woman attempting to smoke methamphetamine inside its trunk. There is no record from inside the tree.

Yes, I caused it to light up.

When it comes to harming a thing, I was always one to go to it. But listen to me: It weren't done out of meanness. It was done out of my own disregard, my own attempt to flee from something into something else. It was the light that was all it was lacking, and I guess I gave it that. The light I mean. And to tell you the truth, it sure was a lovely glow that old tree put up to the night stars. It looked like a like chimney all stocked and heavy with timber, and it smelled like Christmas well into January. I kept muttering, "That tree's older than Jesus, and only God knows its name."

I first saw that Senator Tree when I was twelve years old. We had just moved to Seminole County, and my daddy took Susan and me over to see it one day after church. We ate chicken and slaw in the parking area and then walked over to it through the palmettos and brushy wire-grass. The grass tickled my legs and Susan said, "Sara, this place looks like a garden." And I guess it did. Daddy, Susan, and me was the only ones attending, and after walking about 200 yards, I looked up and there it stood. Like an arrow quivered ground-ward, the tree didn't sway against the wind. It just parked its long barked body in the dirt and seemed to merely put with all things in nature. Like it knew wisdoms, or histories, or something. Anyway, Daddy told us that tree was called a bald cypress and that God himself had planted its kind back among the cedars of Lebanon in the Bible and that God instructed Noah to build his ark out of gopher wood, which was what they called cypress trees back in the Bible days. And build it he did.

That night it happened, I wasn't feeling right. These pipes get to you after a while, and my apartment was crowded with folks unkind and unknowing what it means to feel deeply, so I just slipped into the cool of the night, barefooted. I wasn't missed. My place is only about a mile from The Senator and at first, I didn't plan to go there. I just wanted to circle around, clear my head. But somehow my feet kept walking toward the park, step by step. They were determined. When I finally reached the old tree, I don't know why but I just gazed and gazed on it. Even in evening dark, The Senator was a black arrow that drew all the shadows to it. This place is a lot older than Mickey Mouse and his kin, and something powerful like medicine reached out to me and pushed all the known Orlando back beyond light and beyond revenue. I wanted to get close, to get … I don't know … to get among it … to get into it. I lifted my legs over the chain-link fence and crossed over toward it. I reached and touched the old thing, feeling my hands on its roughy bark. After a minute of groping along its sides, I felt a cleft in The Senator. The opening was narrow and deep and without word I squeezed in. Then the hunger came back to me there in the dark of the darkness. I could almost laugh now thinking about it. There in the belly of The Senator my own belly was letting me know it was time to water my need. I took off my shirt in the black and folded it as neatly as I could on the dry ground. Next, I built a squire-nest of twigs and wood-stuff, and then lit my matches—the whole pack went up.

The kindling caught fast and before I understood, the inside of The Senator was aflame. Before I retreated from the heat, I looked up past my knees and belly, past my breasts and smoking pipe, up through the narrows of the tree. It looked all knotty and ghastly filling up with smoke. But the light. The light. It pushed the shadows from the interior of tree and all of time was swirling in my mind. There was the rush of my self-induced state and there was the power of the flame. I was the source and nest. I was the night and the morning come too soon. And then I fled. And then I fled.

Yes, I caused it to light up.

When it comes to harming a thing, I was always one to go to it. But listen, *again*, to me. It weren't done out of meanness. It was done out of my own disregard, my own attempt to flee from something, into something else. It was the light that was all it was lacking, and I guess I gave it that. The light I mean. And to tell you the truth, *the honest, blood-washed truth*, it sure was a lovely glow that old tree put up to the night stars. It looked like a like chimney all stocked and heavy with timber, and it smelled like Christmas well into January. I kept muttering, "That tree's older than Jesus, and only God *told* me its name."

Coda

For Philip Levine (1928-2015), Mark Strand (1934-2014), Galway Kinnell (1927-2014) Seamus Heaney (1939-2013) and the Rest

The 20th century is folding up its chairs
and calling the band back in from the rain.
So we who've sat so long at its foot and trembled
when the brass and snare boomed like bombs,
have gathered up our blankets and tided away those
ornaments of song for another day
as we watch those players, soaked in years,
break down their cornets and shuffle off under the gazebo.

Scott **Honeycutt** grew up in Virginia and Tennessee. His writing has appeared in *Northwest Ohio History, The Journal of Ecocriticism, Anthology of Appalachian Writers VII, Hartskill Review, Torrid Literature Journal* and other publications. He lives in Johnson City, Tennessee, where he is an Assistant Professor of English at East Tennessee State University. When he is not teaching, Scott enjoys walking the hills of Appalachia and spending time with his family.

www.ingramcontent.com/pod-product-compliance
Lightning Source LLC
LaVergne TN
LVHW091236080426

835509LV00009B/1303